PARANORMAL PLACES

A JOURNEY INTO SOME OF
THE WORLD'S MOST HAUNTED LOCATIONS

FROM AMAZON BESTSELLING AUTHOR OF
REAL GHOST STORIES

EVE S. EVANS

PARANORMAL PLACES

PLACES

Some of the World's most haunted buildings and more.

EVE S EVANS

The following stories are based
on true events. Based does not
intend to mean they are
completely true events.

January © 2020 Eve S. Evans

Cover By: MatYan

DEDICATION:

This book is dedicated my father. I
love you.

This book contains a collaboration of haunted stories based on true events.

The stories in this book are mostly hauntings that have happened around the world with numerous forms of shadow people. Some are legends or stories and some are factual.

Please remember to leave a review after reading.

Follow Eve S. Evans on instagram @eves.evansauthor

Or

@foreverhauntedpodcast

Let me know on Instagram that you wrote a review and I'll send you a free copy of one of my other books!

1 Monte Cristo Homestead

In this tourist attraction that was once an inviting home, rumor has it multiple people have died mysterious accidental deaths with some being alleged as murders.

From these tragedies the homestead is now purported to have abundant paranormal activity on the property itself as well as the residence. With such a gruesome history it leaves little question as why this could be claimed as one of Australia's most haunted places.

The homestead was built in 1885 by Christopher William Crawley. A pioneer as well as a struggling farmer, he soon became a successful Entrepreneur. Crawley raised his four daughters and three sons in this wonderfully built home.

December 14, 1910 Crawley passed at around five o'clock in the evening. It is said that he procured an infection from a starched collar that led to blood poisoning. He was survived by his widow and children.

Widow Crawley resided in the home until her death in 1933 at the age of 92. The home remained in the family until 1948 when it was abandoned and left to caretakers and quickly fell into poor condition.

The home was purchased in 1963 by its current owners who spent a few decades restoring it to its former glory. The homestead is now a place for tours and ghost-seekers.

The spirit of Mrs. Crawley is suggested to be one of many spirits that haunt the halls. Others include a pregnant maid who mysteriously fell to her death from the balcony.

In 1961 a former caretaker was shot to death mysteriously on the property. Also, a stable boy burned alive why sleeping on a bed of hay in the stables.

It even gets weirder. A housekeeper confined their mentally ill son in the outhouse for thirty years.

Lastly, a nanny was carrying a baby girl down the stairs. The nanny swears something pushed the child from her arms. But needless to say, the child fell out of her arms and down the stairs and died. Unexplainable dead, mutilated animals have been found around the property as well.

Talk about a morbid past if I've ever heard one! With so many tragedies there's little doubt as to why so many flock to the property to see for themselves.

People have heard their names being whispered, feelings of being touched, footsteps on the balcony where the maid met her untimely end as well as the feeling of being watched.

2 Eastern State Penitentiary

The Fortress-like Penitentiary was to be one of the world's most famous and costly prisons. It was built in 1829 where those who dwelled might have an opportunity to be remorseful for their crimes.

In solitary, detainees ate, exercised and resided alone. Such excessive measures to keep solitary absolutely unsociable were taken that upon leaving their cells they would be enveloped with a hood.

At present all that remains of the once famous prison is shambles. Disintegrating cell blocks hallow empty watch posts and eerie echoing hallways.

Due to overcrowding solitary became non-existent in 1913. Afterwards two sometimes three convicts at a time shared a cell.

Punishments succeeded those who rebuffed to reform after solitary ended. Prisoners would be subject to freezing baths and dangled from the wall for the whole evening, they would be fastened tightly to chairs as to limit all movement for hours to days on end or were starved.

Some famous names were housed in this prison including Al Capone, and Slick Willie.

The infamous prison was not an execution style confinement, however there were grisly murders that shroud its timeline. Many convicts met their premature end as well as at least two guards. Numerous others, possibly hundreds perished from old age or diseases too.

The soils of Eastern State Penitentiary are rumored to be haunted by souls who met their ruin there, massacred or otherwise. Some of the purported activity includes marching footsteps, terrifying shadow figures, or ghostly merriment.

3 Gettysburg

During the American Civil War, July 1-3 1863 in and around the town of Gettysburg, Pennsylvania around fifty thousand men are said to have died between Confederate and Union Soldiers. It is said to be one of the bloodiest battles in American History.

Although the battle alone would entice paranormal activity due to the volume of mass casualties, other spots in Gettysburg also attribute to rumored activity in the area.

Devil's Den is an area of the battle which saw heavy combat on the battle's second day. It is now rumored to be one of the most haunted areas of the battlefield. It is also said this area surpasses Gettysburg as a whole with its paranormal phenomenon.

Devil's Den can also be known as The Valley Of Death. Devil's Den did not get it's name from the war however, it was deemed this long before. Prior to the Civil War, Devil's Den was the location of a Native American brawl "Battle of the Crows."

A creek running between Devil's Den and one of its mountains is called Bloody Run. So many were slaughtered there that the creek literally ran crimson.

The battlefield phenomenon has several unexplained phenomena. Cameras, cell phones or other electronic devices are said to not turn on or refuse to work when they work just fine in other parts of the town.

A disheveled man has been spotted barefoot and poorly dressed. He has reportedly spoken to people at times or gestured and then vanished into thin air.

Other activity consists of but is not limited to the faint smell of cigars, phantom rifle discharges, batteries being drained from phones or vehicles or apparitions on the battlefield itself.

The Jennie Wade House is another haunted area of Gettysburg. It is purportedly one of America's scariest haunted houses. Jennie Wade was the one and only civilian casualty. She was hit by a stray bullet while she baked in her kitchen. Wade died on the battle's last day. She is said to still remain in the home roaming around with several children spirits. Loud unexplained noises, a voice of a young child, sudden cold spots on the upper level of the home are a few occurrences.

Sachs Covered Bridge is another paranormal hot spot in Gettysburg. Back in the days of battle, the fleeing Confederate Army crossed it. Rumor has it that three hangings took place at this bridge of army deserters. Those who have visited the bridge have had experiences such as: Hearing unexplainable voices, being touched by something that isn't there, smelling burning tobacco as well as spirits.

The Gettysburg Hotel, another ghostly hot spot in the area, was once a hospital during the Civil War. A nurse that tended to the wounded during the horrific days of the battle has been known to rummage through rooms and belongings of its guests. An unknown soldier has also been spotted. Supposedly he passed away in the hospital and still wanders around the hotel spooking its patrons.

The Farnsworth House Inn, a charming bed and breakfast may be more spooky than charming on occasion. Confederate snipers were sheltered in this location during the Civil War. The fatal shot that killed Jennie Wade is said to have come from this location. Guests have heard singing originating from the basement on occasion as well as inexplicable noises coming from the attic.

Dobbin House Tavern was once a stop on the underground railroad. Partake here and you just might spot the spirits of former slaves. It is said they wander the building.

Gettysburg College also hosts some activity. During the war it was a field hospital for both sides. A story dated back to the early 20th century is the most haunting. Two college personnel walked on an elevator and pressed the button of their chosen floor. Instead of going to where it was instructed, the elevator took them to the basement. A little on edge already from the elevator malfunctioned, they were shocked at what they saw when the elevator doors finally opened. The basement was a bloody mess with doctor's working anxiously on patients. The elevator finally moved them to another floor, and they told a security guard. With a security guard in toe, they returned to the basement to find it completely unoccupied.

4 The Willard Library

This elegant Victorian style building may not be as elegant as it puts off as it has multiple sightings of apparitions. One in particular has been seen quite often and dubbed "The Grey Lady". Some believe she may be the daughter of the founder Louise Carpenter.

Many other unexplained events and sightings have occurred. Several library employees have reported seeing an entity. And after having a security alarm tripped, officers arrived to find what looked like two apparitions in an upstairs library window.

Every October the library hosts ghost tours and multiple people come looking for "The Grey Lady." Is "The Grey Lady" actually the daughter of Willard Carpenter? Or is she some other lost spirit just seeking knowledge for eternity beyond the walls of the library?

Other unexplained events that have been reported are phantom smells such as perfume, unexplainable noises or banging, furniture being in odd locations from where it was last, books being moved about, random items found in the library that weren't there before, areas of extreme cold throughout the building, and on occasion water has turned on or off by itself.

5 Wicklow Gaol

Wicklow Gaol is located in Wicklow, Ireland. It is a significant prison which earned infamy for the cruel treatment of its prisoners as well as the viciousness of the wardens.

In 1924 Wicklow Gaol finally ceased running and was deserted. Over the years the building, being neglected, fell into ruin.

Over time, Wicklow Gaol is said to now be haunted by the souls of prisoners that died within it's crumbling walls. Some visitors have seen a man strolling out of cell 19, a emerald-like mist gliding around, the echoes of children sobbing, and a woman in a cloak straying around the main floor.

6 The Leap Castle

One of Ireland's most notoriously haunted places, the Leap Castle is located in Coolderry, Ireland. Ghost hunters as well as television shows have shown their interest in this haunted local.

The castle claims a very intriguing and somewhat confusing past. Nonetheless, it is a gruesome past at that. Originally named Leim Ui Bhanain, ("Leap of the O'Bannons) the Leap Castle was built atop of lands formerly occupied by druids who used the

land for commencement
ceremonies.

The O'Bannon's were a
wealthy family from County
Tipperary, however they were
docile to another family, the
O'Carrolls. As the legend goes,
two of the O'Bannon brothers were
fighting over the power of their
family. In order to determine who
would be in charge, they
challenged each other to jump
from a rock in which the castle was
to be constructed. Whoever lived
from such a jump would be
allowed to govern the family and
oversee the castle's construction.

The O'Carrolls seized the
castle from the O'Bannons not
long after this. Legend has it that
at the hands of the O'Carrolls,
much bloodshed, fear and terror
came to the castle staining it to the
core.

The O'Carrolls torment and murderous rage throughout the years of the castle is said to be one of legend or lore. However multiple spirits are said to roam the castle.

The Red Lady is said to haunt the castle. According to legend, she was raped by the O'Carrolls and caged. Once she gave birth to her baby, the O'Carrolls slaughtered the child. Grief stricken; the red lady took her own life with a knife.

The Oubliette, the castle's dungeon was used to slaughter numerous amounts of people. With only one way of entrance, an opening in the ceiling it was impossible to escape once being thrown down there. Some landed on a spike and died, others suffered from injuries or starvation until they perished.

During a renovation, it was shocking just how many skeletal remains were found in this "secret dungeon". One hundred and fifty human remains were obtained from the Oubliette. It was such a job that it took three cart heaps in order to haul off all of the skeletal remains.

With that many murdered souls buried deep in the heart of the castle, why wouldn't it be haunted? So many poor souls suffering such horrendously painful deaths.

7 Old Government House

The Old Government House in Parramatta Park is one of Australia's oldest colonial buildings. With its age and history there is not much wonder why this location could be haunted. However, the ghosts here are not particularly "unfriendly".

A woman apparition many have seen have dubbed her "The Lady in Blue" and she is sometimes seen with companion dog. Occasionally she appears in the upstairs window. Most presume she is possibly the daughter of Governor Bligh.

Another spirit often seen around is assumed Lady Fitzroy after she died in a horse and cart accident on December 7, 1847. Her lifeless body was brought into the foyer of the building and many refuse to stand in that exact spot.

This beautiful Homestead is located about an hour from Central Sydney. It is said to have been built between 199 and 1816. In the early 1990's the building began offering a popular ghost tour. This tour still runs today on Friday evenings. For being one of the oldest remaining public structures it still holds it's charm.

Inside the Old Government House is what has been dubbed "The Blue Room". Much activity is centered around this room. Maybe it is a portal or a sensitive area, no one can be sure. "The Blue

Room" is located at the top of the original wooden staircase. The room has been painted blue (hence its name).

Nearby "The Blue Room" hangs a picture of Mary Bligh, the daughter of the Governor. Some believe she is "The Lady in Blue". Sometimes she has been seen walking the hall just outside "The Blue Room" with her companion dog in her arms just as in the painting.

One day a workman was isolated in a semi-lit room connecting a chandelier when he peered over at one of the windows and was shocked to see an immaterial face staring back at him. He looked to the window next to it only to see the same creepy face in that window as well. This was one of the first ghost sightings of "The Old Government House."

Other mysterious things besides "The Blue Lady" have happened over the years at historic building. Some have had the luxury to chat with the "Lady in Blue", others have heard unexplainable voices throughout the dwelling. Another person visually saw the apparition of a man staying beside him in a hallway.

8 Old Quarantine Station

The Old Quarantine Station features its own power source, hospital, morgue, telephone trade, reservoir, post office and a few other numerous buildings on the surrounding paved roads.

During its quarantine days, some of its occupants were required to endure long dreadful voyages on infectious ridden ships.

After arriving at the quarantine station, the atmosphere was gloomy at best. Most people were miserable and suffering with disease everywhere.

Some of the first ghost sightings date back more than a century. Wandering spirits through some of the wards. After investigating whatever ghostly apparition has all but disappeared.

Light bulbs sometimes will explode randomly during tours, unexplained cold spots, the feeling of being touched or tapped on, and of course ghostly figures that can't be explained away as anything else but a phenomenon.

9 Studley Park House

One of Camden's most haunted buildings is a cornerstone of Camden Golf Course. From the outside its lavish Victorian Italianate architecture is breath-taking. Lavish green surrounds the "country estate" building. To this day, photos don't seem to do the beauty of this building the justice it deserves.

However beautiful and serene from the outside, several stories of tragedies exist surrounding its history. As it is said, in 1909 a boy drowned in the dam. Another story is from 1939 when the then title holder, Arthur Gregory suffered the loss of his son to appendicitis.

In 2010, while the roof was under restoration, a hangman's noose was found from within the steeple.

Some have reported disembodied voices from the rooftop or other locations. Others have seen entities in the windows as if they are peering out overlooking the serene landscaping.

10 Prince Henry Hospital

In 1881 this building was established originally as The Coast Hospital. In 1934 its name was modified to honor a visit from HRH Henry, the Duke of Gloucester.

Constructed away from the main city, its objective was to treat ailments such as transmittable diseases. It did in fact treat such diseases as leprosy, typhoid, smallpox and a few others during its days.

During both world wars, veterans were also handled there. Nurses would tend to their injuries or ailments from the war.

Soon, years passed by and the threat of communicable disease was limited. The hospital was then renovated to be a modern hospital of General Medicine.

Through the years it even had its own graveyard. Unkempt, and more likely deserted at this point it is said to contain well over one thousand resting souls.

Gracie, a disturbed woman is said to be one of the entities that plagues the hospital. It is said that Gracie was a Germaphobe. After being touched she would instantly rinse her hands or pull back repulsively. The story says that her circumstances of death remain a mystery. Her spirit is often perceived on Delany Ward.

The spirit of a young boy also haunts B-Block. Sometimes he is in the stairwell stumbling nurses or other persons using it. His laughter can be heard on occasion as well as if he is overjoyed with his pranks. Some say they have not seen him but can feel his presence from time to time. No one is sure who the little boy could possibly be.

A male entity much older than the boy is said to wander the halls at night. His shadow has been seen but not anything else. It is said he is not a pleasant spirit but an ominous one.

As of modern day, the hospital no longer functions. However, a shell of structures does remain of the center.

11 Boise State Murder House

Once reported to be the location of a brutal murder in 1987, it is now a frat house. It is said that a man murdered multiple people, mutilated their bodies and scattered them around the area.

Some of the paranormal or unexplained phenomenon that surrounds this house is blood spots that appear out of thin air and disappear just the same. There has also been some reports of blinds on the windows being opened and shut by themselves.

12 City Hall Brisbane

Since the 1950's the city hall has been purportedly haunted. At least, some people say it is. In the 1940's a caretaker supposedly committed suicide around room 302 (which is actually a small cluster of rooms). Some have heard footsteps or felt guarded by some sinister presence in the area.

Abandoned after being used as a photographic darkroom, the city hall finally had reached its peak of afterlife activity.

13 Old Changi Hospital

As of the present, overgrowth swallows up the remains of the building as it sits empty at the end of Halton Road. Old Changi Hospital is purportedly one of the most haunted places in Singapore.

Since being constructed it has kept quite the reputation for hauntings and "the unexplainable".

Bloody apparitions of soldiers have been seen wandering the hallways. A young boy spirit has been seen sitting and just staring. Disembodied screaming and voices have also been heard in the dwelling.

A "black aura" has been seen as well as abrupt loud noises. Some stories even relay being touched by something unseen, whether a presence or "spirit hands".

The gothic-like structure of
Moundsville Penitentiary was
opened in 1876. Originally built to
contain only 480 prisoners, but by
the 1930's it was at 2,400-person
capacity. On occasion three
convicts would be held in a
minuscule five by seven cell at the
same time.

In the late 1800's
Moundsville was in charge of
executions for the state of West
Virginia. Eighty-five men were

either electrocuted or hung in this penitentiary.

In 1986 it was declared by the West Virginia Supreme Court that the petite cells were a harsh punishment and ordered the prisons closure.

Moundsville has numerous locations of "hot spots", areas where activity is at a peak. Death row, a chapel, and shower cages are all said to be "hot spots".

Some people claim that the dwelling is a place of residual hauntings. Where the spirits of the tortured and murdered inmates replay their final days and years over and over again. If this claim is true, which I'm sure we will never know for sure, I believe that they have paid for their crimes to the fullest. Not only to be imprisoned during life, but to be stuck in a loop for all eternity.

15 Adelaide Street Butcher Shop

In Brisbane behind an Arcade there used to stand a butcher's shop. The L-shaped shop had two sections. One being where the meat was cleaved and prepared and another where the patrons were served.

As the legend goes, the butcher had an apprentice helping him out in the shop. Suddenly they got into an argument. A meat cleaver was hurled, and the apprentice was killed.

On occasion some have claimed to hear the sounds of disembodied voices arguing, screams or echoes of a scuffle.

16 Wan Chai House

A prominent Chinese business man purchased and leased this home in 1920 shortly after it was built.

It is said that in the 1940's after the Japanese invaded and inhabited Hong Kong, the house was used as a military lair of wickedness.

Some sources suggest that many local women were taken by the Japanese soldiers and hauled inside only to be raped, tormented, slaughtered or beheaded. Some stories say that the soldiers left the deceased outside to decompose in the streets.

Apparitions of headless, bloody women have been seen from inside the home. Their screams are also said to be heard and apparently will reverberate in your ears for minutes to even hours.

A male entity has also been spotted on the location as well. It appears he is dressed in all black and strolls around the building. It is unsure who the man could possibly be.

17 Calcutta Public Library

Being dubbed one of the largest libraries in India, the library was built in 1836. Renamed in 1891 to Imperial Library, only to be changed again when the Government of India took over after independence to National Public Library.

The now public library holds over 2,270,000 books, 3,200 manuscripts and 86,000 maps.

It is assumed that the apparition of the wife of Lord Metcalfe roams the halls of the library. Being a meticulous woman, sometimes people feel as if they are being observed, or as if someone is watching them intently to see if they put all of their books back in place.

Another legend that has been circled around is one of a few laborers. During some renovations on the building it is believed they died. Some have said that over the years their spirits have been seen in the building.

18 Bigges Bridge

The Bigge's Bridge's construction began in 1823 and stretched all the way into 1825. Convicts transported local sandstone to construct the bridge. Before the town of Richmond grew larger the bridge was named Bigge's Bridge after John Bigges the man who commissioned the bridge. After Richmond flourished and grew, the bridge was renamed Richmond Bridge.

Constructed between Hobart and Port Arthur, it made the

transport of prisioners much easier. This gave to the nickname the 'convict trail'.

Since 1825 their have been few alterations to the bridge as it is believed to be one of the first bridges built in Australia. A protected heritage site, the bridge is still in use today.

An ex-prisioner named George Grover had been sent from Australia to England for stealing was often referred to as hostile and unpleasant.

In 1829 he had finished his sentence in full and was free to do as he wished. He chose to stay in the area and work as a lash-bearer.

Later that year the bridge was to be rebuilt. Again, they used prisoners as laborers, but this time Grover was in charge of overseeing the convicts. Being the hostile man he was, he was incredibly cruel to the inmates. On some occasions he even treated them as if they were his own personal slaves. He seemed to gain a sick thrill out of it. He would lash them even if they hadn't done anything amiss, or whip them as if they were livestock.

The convicts grew to loathe Grover. Authorities saw Grover however as an asset and upped his pay due to his effectiveness on the inmates. Meanwhile Grover continued to basque in the control he had over the prisoners.

One evening Grover got plastered. He was being belligerent and bothering his neighbors so was sent away. After wandering around the town, he finally settled on the Richmond Bridge and passed out.

The story goes that once the inmates heard that Grover had

passed out on the bridge, they were joyous for a chance at retribution.

Once at the bridge they began beating him senseless. It is said Grover woke up just before he was hit with a pickaxe to the skull then hurled off the bridge like garbage.

Needless to say, it is assumed that Grover haunts the Richmond Bridge. He has been spotted as a shady figure strolling or standing near or on the bridge. Sometimes he gazes at people.

Some accounts claim that Grover's ghost is just as sinister in death as he was alive. They believe on occasion his ghost has pursued them home and plague their homes for a period of time before returning back to the bridge.

19 Rose Hall

The Legend of The White Witch of Rose Hall is just that, a legend. However, it makes for a thriller of a story. This legend centers around Annie Palmer who supposedly is the "White Witch".

I will tell you the legend but first I will tell you the more factual story.

Annie Palmer was born Annie Mary Paterson with Jamaican Scots heritage. She was brought up with no nanny and never resided in Haiti, nor did she ever train in voodoo.

John Rose Palmer did become her husband in 1820. He was her one and only husband. Their time at the rose hall was peaceful, simple and quite short. However, neither died in the residence.

Rose Hall became too high with debt and was eventually handed off down the family line until it sat vacant for 130 years.

Now, onto the legend that has so many intrigued and even tourists salivating at a chance to tour the Rose Hall.

An eightieth-century plantation manor house and one of few remaining slave-run manors in Jamaica. Most of the other manors were burnt to the ground after the Great Jamaican Slave revolt of 1831-1832.

According to the story (which has numerous versions) Annie Palmer moved with her family to Haiti when she was around ten years old. Being trusted in the hands of a Haitian nanny, she dabbled in voodoo.

When Annie's parents succumbed to yellow fever, Annie was left to be raised by her Haitian nanny. In which over the years became a master at voodoo.

Shortly after she turned eighteen, in search of a wealthy husband to wed, Annie moved to Jamaica. Soon after her arrival she met John Palmer who by that time was the owner of Rose Hall.

Folklore has it that not long after they wed Annie began to bore of her husband. It was not long before she began to take slaves as secret lovers. On one occasion John supposedly caught her in the act, beating her with a racing crop.

According to legend this provoked Annie to poison John's coffee as he was found dead the very next day.

After John had passed Annie inherited the entire Rose Hall. Continuing to have slaves as lovers, Annie reigned over Rose Hall. If she tired of a slave, she would simply murder them. On a steady basis she would brutalize her slaves or kill any that annoyed her in any way.

According to legend she regularly practiced voodoo at Rose Hall while mistreating and torturing slaves. This dubbed her the name "The White Witch of Rose Hall" by the slaves.

After two more marriages, both ending in murder for money, one stabbed in the chest in his chest in his sleep and the other strangled to death, her demise began. Takoo one of her slave lovers had supposedly helped her with atleast one of the crimes.

Not long after, Annie fell for an Englishman named Robert. Robert did not love Annie. He was smitten by Takoo's granddaughter.

Broken-hearted Annie used a voodoo spell called "old hige" on the granddaughter to get her out of the way. The spell was intended to cause the person on whom it was cast to slowly shrivel and perish. Which eventually did happen. Takoo being grief-stricken and so full of hatred towards Annie, strangled her to death.

Legend finishes after the slaves buried Annie's body in a deep hole on the property. All of her earthly possessions were burned to remove her attachment to this world.

In order to provide comfortable means of lodging to those traveling by train, the Fort Garry Hotel was constructed by the Grand Trunk Pacific Railway.

Adored by travelers, the hotel became exactly what the hope for it had been. With exquisite architecture, lavish design, and twelve stories tall it accommodates three hundred and forty rooms for lodgers.

For the era of the Hotel, it was unique. Each room had a

personal bathroom which was uncommon for the time period. Most other lodging options had communal bathrooms. The Hotel held many other features that seemed "top-class" of it's time. A ballroom, a concert hall, music room, bakery and many more. The location also had its own well and press. With so much lavish options it seemed to be a city within a city itself.

A residual haunting has been rumored at the Fort Garry. Legend has it that a woman received unfavorable news of the love of her life had tragically died. Riddled with despair and heartbreak she cried until there were no tears left. All that came were empty sobs. She wandered over to a closet determined to meet him on the other side and hung herself.

Because so many have seen or heard her, it is rumored

that she never reunited with her love on the other side. Her spirit is trapped to wander the hotel for eternity.

Other unexplained activity in the hotel has been sounds. Some can be heard throughout the establishment; others have been crying or mourning. And sudden phantom conversing.

21 Hastings House
Turf Club

The two-story white home boasted a stone and black stairway, a hall and rooms on each floor.

In the 1930's, George Williams resided in the home. His greatest passions and hobbies were horse racing or horses. Some would even say he put his love for horses and racing above his own family.

Pride was his favorite horse. Being one of his most profitable competitors, Pride also brought him not only wealth but fame.

After some time, Pride's winning streaks began to cease. The horse no longer brought him fame but shame. After one last race defeat, Pride was found shot dead at the racetrack.

Many have said to see the spirit of Pride leaping or strolling around the track.

Warren Hastings was impeached in 1787 and was charged with crime and corruption. The indictments followed him for years until finally he was acquitted in 1795.

Warren Hastings was the original owner of the Hastings house and had it built for himself. In August 1818 Warren Hastings died.

Since the ownerships over the years a few unexplainable

phenomenon has occurred. A phantom carriage was reportedly seen racing towards the Hastings House. The apparition of Warren Hastings is also rumored to have been seen. And crazed laughter can be heard on occasion supposedly from Warren Hastings.

22 Shelbourne Hotel

A playful young girl is rumored to haunt this lavish hotel. As stories go, on multiple occasions guests have fled a specific room terrified and whimpering in fear.

Many accounts of sinks, showers or bathtubs running by themselves. The sounds of giggles have also been noticed.

It is said the young girl, Mary Masters died from cholera in the hotel. Since her death the strange activity in the hotel has occurred.

Is Mary Masters haunting the Shelbourne? Or is it just another legend?

23 Garth Homestead

The Garth Homestead originally built of sandstone is now a disintegrating pile of shambles. It is said to be one of the most haunted spots in Tasmania even with it being reduced to rubbish.

The Garth Homestead was originally constructed by prisoners but contracted by and Englishman out of love. It was a romance beginning to a tragic story.

The English man left behind his one and only love to build a lavish two-story home for them.

He promised to come back and retrieve her once the construction was completed.

Once the walls were plastered and the ceilings were complete, he did just that. He traveled back to collect his love, or so he thought. Once he arrived his heart was shattered into pieces. He learned she had married another man and fallen for him while he was away building this dream house.

It is then said that the English man disheartened, returned to the not yet completed project. He then killed himself in the courtyard.

The story continues with new owners and a young girl and her nanny. The nanny ruled with a strict thumb. She would warn the child if she did not behave, she would be tossed down the well. On one occasion the nanny even held her by ankle over the well to prove her threat real.

The young girl eventually did misbehave and expecting the inevitable punishment threw herself in the well. Shame ridden; the nanny tried to come to her aide. However, when trying to recover the child she too fell into the well to die along side the girl in the freezing waters.

In the late 1830's, Charles Peters a Scotsman took over the property including the Garth House. Seeing some charm in the property he decided to move his family into the home.

1840 came around and so did tragedy for Charles Peters and his wife. His two-year-old daughter had caught a blaze watching house staff make jams over a fire. She ran into the parlor screaming seeking any sort of assistance. Unfortunately, the burns were too much to recover from and Ann Peters was buried in a small grave on the property.

Some say these are all stories with not much truth, others say they really happened. But one thing is for sure that the house is no longer inhabited but an abandoned crumbling mess.

The house has had a few fires over its time as well. Some exchanges in ownership, and now sits a neglected pile of ruins.

24 Carey Mansion

The Carey Mansion, also known as Seaview Terrace, was once located in Washington D.C. Edson Bradley the builder and liquor mogul decided to move his entire house to Newport.

This was not an easy job by any means. The entire house was undone and relocated. The house now sits along the Cliff Walk in Newport.

A few rumors of activity have surfaced. Unexplainable

voices, random thumping, or other noises.

Mrs. Bradley, the wife of the original owner is said to play her favorite organ in the house from time to time. Some assume she never wanted to leave her extravagant house even after death.

The Great Hall has had some sightings of apparitions wandering. Some have claimed to hear footsteps when there is no one around to make the noise.

25 Whepstead Manor

Gilbert Burnett moved into his new residence "Fernbourne" in 1889. The house was spacious. Adorned with two levels and a expansive attic. He would not reside their long before liquidating assets and selling the home he now called "Whepstead Manor".

A private hospital 'Bayview' in the Cleveland area took over residence of the Whepstead Manor in 1937.

In the 1960's Whepstead Manor again, became something different. This time it was a nursing home. In 1973 the Whepstead Manor became privately owned and not much else is known about the ownership.

Through all the changes the home has overcome it is said to be haunted. A young woman has been seen that is assumed to be Gilbert's wife from the overwhelming aroma of lavender has been smelled and this was her favorite perfume. On a few occasions there have been sightings of a man in the attic. Some have seen the image of a man randomly appear in a mirror.

Two other spirits have been seen. They are children. It is believed they are Gilbert's children. His daughter vanished without a trace and was never found. And his son, as legend has it was plagued with a shriveled leg.

The boy is said to perch or peer around the staircase.

In most cases the sightings themselves seem mostly innocent. It appears the spirits, if any, are more curious than violent. Sometimes there has been reports of slightly odd occurrences that were not so innocent. Hair is said to have been yanked, a few objects tossed by something invisible and occasionally odd stains appearing and vanishing without explanation.

Is the Whepstead Manor (now supposed restaurant) really haunted? Or is it all just legend? You decide.

Haunted

THE BOAT

My mother Elena suffered from Epilepsy. She had it as long as I could remember. Now grown and on my own, I felt it was my duty to take her in and keep an eye on her. You never knew when it would happen and there's no known cure for it.

Some people are lucky, and only have it occurring for a few years, and others have it their entire lives. My mom was an unfortunate case.

It was around two in the morning and a clatter coming from my mother's room woke me up.

Hastily I ran to investigate. My mother was tangled in her bedding obviously having a seizure and suffocating. I did my best to untangle her while dialing 911.

I performed CPR on her until paramedics arrived. Once they were in the house, I felt like I was in an ant farm. People were running here and shuffling there. I was shoved out of the way so they could work on her. I was numb. Delirious and numb.

I sat on the bottom stair, which was right outside her bedroom and just stared off into space. The only thought I could recollect is *this better not be how it ends. This cannot be how it ends.*

After a few minutes that felt like numb hours, they did get her breathing again. Immediately they transported her to the hospital.

I had stayed behind to get dressed. I was still in my boxers and no shirt on.

In my room, still numb, fumbling through my drawers for something quick and easy to throw on, the phone rang. It was my aunt.

I answered thoughtlessly and exhausted.

She was breathless and sounded groggy. "Jake you will not believe the dream I just had. I had a dream I was on a boat with your mother. We were sailing off into the golden bright sunset and then she turned to me and told me she was dead. It felt so real."

I choked on my words and just sat there in silence. I stared at the wall in front of me and I knew. Well, I was pretty sure I knew.

This was too much of a coincidence to not have some truth.

I told her what had just happened, and she agreed to meet me at the hospital immediately.

I tugged on my shoes, grabbed my keys and drove in a blur to the hospital.

As I expected, the doctor was waiting for me when I arrived. His facial expression told me all I needed to know. She was gone.

The chaplain escorted my Aunt and I to a room and we got counseled. I know I'm supposed to feel better after talking with them, but I didn't.

I sat there with my elbows on my knees, my head in my hands and tried to stay calm. Tried to make sense of the words being directed at me. But I felt like I was trying to understand Charlie

Brown's teacher. None of it made much sense.

I didn't get home until around six in the morning. The horizon was already peeking light through the valley.

I threw my keys in my key dish and landed with a belly-flop on the couch. There was no need to sleep in my bed, this would do just fine.

I grabbed the blanket off of the back of the couch and tucked myself under it like hiding from the world would shield the pain I was feeling. The absolute shock and loss overwhelming my entire body.

Soon I drifted off. I dreamt of an ocean. The waters edges were highlighted by golden sunlight. It was beautiful.

Birds cawed in the distance and the lapping noises of the ocean were soothing. I was on a boat. *The* boat. My Aunt's boat.

My mom sat next to me smiling, watching me watch the water and the sky. She put the back of her hand up and grazed my cheek.

"I guess you know," she said and stared off into the sunset.

"I guess I know," I replied.

NAME CALLING

My parents divorced when I was ten. I suffered from severe anxiety and depression. In the midst of dealing with my mental health, strange things began to happen at home.

One night I was up late, it was about one in the morning. I was having trouble sleeping on some of my medications. I was watching television quietly as to not bother my mom.

I heard a man's voice say my name. I sat there for a few minutes and heard nothing more, so I brushed it off and eventually went to sleep.

A few nights later I was up late again having trouble sleeping. Again, I was watching television and it was around one in the morning. I heard someone call my name again, this time it was louder and sounded closer. As if whoever said it was standing in the doorway of my room.

I turned my side lamp on and saw no one. I went to my mom's room and they were both sleeping. I fought off a shudder and went back to my room and shut the door.

It was a few days before anything else happened, so I had forgotten all about my name being called.

Lounging in my bed snacking on some chips it was around midnight. I had my door very lightly cracked instead of open like I usually leave it.

The door began to creak and open by itself. Then the room had to drop at least ten degrees in temperature. I sat there holding a chip up to lips just staring at the door.

Then I heard what sounded like scuffing footsteps on the hardwood floor towards my bed. Not normal thump, thump steps. Like someone sliding their shoes or feet on the floor as they walked.

I kept eyeing towards the door and there was nothing there. No ghostly figure, no mist, nothing. But still I heard scuffling getting closer to my bed.

I finally jumped out of bed and ran out into the hallway and screamed for my mom.

She ran out into the hallway frazzled and took me under her arm and held me. She led me back to my room (which was the last place I wanted to be) and told me there was nothing to be afraid of.

This activity went on for years. My mom didn't believe me, my dad didn't believe me. They thought I was just acting out because of the divorce or it was some sort of side effect of the medication I was on.

They got me prescribed some sleeping pills to help me fall asleep and that helped somewhat. I guess it was better to sleep through whatever was happening than be awake for it.

It was about two years before I quit hearing the voice calling my name in the middle of the night. My mom got relocated to a different city with her job and it stopped.

I never told her about it, mostly because I started thinking that I was crazy.

EYELESS

Our old house was spooky. There was no doubt in my mind.

In the beginning, the activity was minor. My keys were moved from where I had left them on the table, floorboards creaking behind us while watching television.

But one night I had to work late. I came home and relieved the babysitter. Then I went into my daughter's room to tuck her in.

She was sound asleep. I gave her a kiss on the head and headed to my bedroom to take a shower before bed.

I'm in the shower and I hear a scratching noise. Like branches on a window. Only thing is, my bathroom doesn't have a window.

So, I open the shower door and peer out to see if my daughter had gotten out of bed and what she was doing. I did not see anyone.

I decided to turn the water off and get out of the shower so I could further investigate.

I'm in my room dressing and I hear the noise again. This time it sounds like its coming from the hallway.

I hastily throw my shirt on and go out into the hallway. Again nothing.

I'm pretty rattled and confused at what is happening. This noise is not something I have ever heard in my house before.

I decide to check on my daughter again incase someone broke in or something. She's tucked in the corner of her bed whimpering.

I'm asking her over and over what is wrong, and she just keeps staring at a corner in the ceiling then darting her eyes towards me and back to the ceiling. Her eyes are filled with pure terror.

I make my way over to her, sit on her bed and take her in my arms. I start rocking her and putting my fingers through her hair telling her everything is ok.

"Did you have a nightmare honey?" I had asked.

She pointed towards the ceiling in the corner with a shaky finger and said, "Don't you see the man with no eyes right there mom?"

My eyes had to bug out of my head. I hadn't turned any lights on in her room. All there was, was her night light.

I had to be the protector. So, I slowly turned my head in the direction of her finger and looked at the ceiling. I did not see a man with no eyes, but I did see a black mist up by the ceiling.

I scooped my daughter up and brought her into my room. That's where we both slept with the door locked (like it would keep out a spirit).

For several years my daughter has told me about the man with no eyes. He does nothing to harm her she says he just stares at her in the middle of the night. Sometimes he's on the ceiling and sometimes he is in her closet.

SCARED TO DEATH

I worked at night as a
911 operator. On this particular
day I received the weirdest call of
my career.

A woman called in
around two in the morning terrified.
She said there was a ghost in her
house and her and her daughter
were terrified to leave the bedroom
to get out of the house.

In the background of the call
you could literally hear things
smashing in the distance. I'm not

one to believe in ghosts so this call threw me for quite the loop.

I dispatched help to their location and kept asking her if it was possible that someone broke in. She kept telling me no. She was sure. She had seen the thing and so had her daughter that it was not of this world.

I'm trying to keep her calm until help arrives and she starts screaming that its now at their bedroom door jangling the doorknob, that it's going to get in.

Again, I'm saying anything I can to keep her calm. Then you hear the sound of the doorknob falling on the floor and I hear her draw in a breath and whisper, "Oh my god."

Then the line goes dead.

I asked for an update after emergency crews arrived. It still spooks me to this day.

They had to break in the front door because everything was locked. No intruder in the house.

They found the mom and daughter in the bedroom. The daughter was whimpering under the bed, and the mom was deceased on the floor.

The doorknob was laying right inside the bedroom on the floor.

When they asked the daughter what had happened, she said, "It was the scary man who only appears at night."

The mom died of Broken Heart Syndrome. So basically, the woman was scared to death.

Still gives me chills to this day.

It was my birthday weekend. I had begged my parents to let me invite over a few friends and tent camp in our backyard. I was ten after all, and big enough to be in the backyard with a few friends for just one night.

Hesitantly, my mother agreed. My father was to check on us multiple times throughout the evening just to make sure everything was going smoothly.

My house was literally two houses away from an old cemetery built in the late 1800's. And I was determined to get a rise out of my friends by telling ghost stories.

In the late afternoon I helped my father set up the tent. He kept reminding me to stay in the yard and no funny business because he would be checking on us at random times. I nodded and agreed, I had no intentions of leaving the yard.

My friends and I jumped on my trampoline for the next few hours. We went inside, grabbed some popcorn and some sodas and brought it back out to the tent and readied our beds.

As it began getting dark my parents came out to say goodnight and make sure we had all that we needed in the tent for the evening.

When my parents had gone back inside, we turned our

flashlights on and talked about some of the girls at school.

Brian was the scaredy cat of the bunch and I was extremely excited to scare him with a really good story.

He kept telling us he was hearing rustling in the bushes. Eddie, my other friend unzipped the tent once to check and there was nothing there.

We pretty much shrugged it off as Brian being scaredy-cat Brian and continued to chat awhile longer.

When it was really good and dark, I suggested telling ghost stories. Eddie was elated, Brian gulped and tried to hide his wide, unsure eyes.

We patted Brian on the shoulder and assured him they would not be too scary. He nodded and agreed. We let him go first.

His story was not the best attempt and a scare-all. Eddie and I kept exchanging bored glances and patiently waited for him to finish.

Once Brian had finished, Eddie and I faked shocked and patted Brian on the shoulder.

"Good one," I said. "Ok Eddie, your turn."

Eddie began a story about a vacant house on the outskirts of town where a little boy had died. The little boy's family moved away a few years after his death from the trauma. The little boy roamed the streets of the town searching and hoping to find his family.

This boy was not a nice little boy. He was angry with his family for leaving him to rot alone in the house forever. He would terrorize people on the streets late at night.

Shove them in front of oncoming cars, trip them so that they fell, those types of things.

When Eddie was done, I gave him a thumbs up. "Good one dude."

Brian looked at Eddie and then looked back at me. He knew I was the best storyteller out of all of us. I'm pretty sure he was scared to hear what my story was going to be about.

Before I had a chance to start my story however, the zipper on the tent slowly started unzipping itself.

All three of us sat there, flashlights pointed upwards at our chins in horror. We just listened as it kept unzipping, just slowly enough to hear.

I tried to calm down by telling the guys it was probably just my dad checking in on us. I got up to prove my point.

When I finished unzipping the tent and stuck my head out, no one was there. Quickly I pushed myself back into the tent and sat there frozen.

Both boys looked at me expectantly.

"Well?" Brian nudged big bulging eyes. "Is it your dad?"

With all my might I shook my head no and sat there with my arms wrapped around myself.

"What are you waiting for then!" Eddie screamed, "I'm going inside!"

Both boys took off to my house, I was following close behind. I kept turning my head and glancing behind me for some person to be following at my heels.

The only thing I saw was at the gate of the cemetery. It looked like a little boy was standing there holding a teddy bear in one hand staring directly at us.

SICK DAY

It all started on a day I wasn't feeling very well and stayed home from work. My wife and I had just moved into a house about a month prior.

I had all of it. The chills, then the sweats, kept vomiting. I was in and out of sleep with a fever.

Finally falling into a deep sleep facing the wall I felt the tiniest bit of relief and snoozed.

Half in and out of sleep I heard our bedroom door creak open. I was so out of it and groggy I didn't even seem to register the door being opened and what it meant since my wife was at work and not at home.

A searing pain in my back fully woke me with a yelp. It felt like something had scratched my back... hard.

As I jumped out of bed, I could hear what sounded like muffled laugher and light footsteps receding in the hallway. Sounded almost like the pitter-patter of child footsteps.

Immediately I ducked into the bathroom to check my back. I lifted my shirt and there were three long scratches from my shoulder blades to my lower back.

I was shocked. Obviously, this couldn't be my imagination. Sure, I was sick, but now I had proof… on my body. I slowly lowered my shirt walked back into the bedroom shut and locked the door.

I half waited for my wife to get home, so I did not have to be alone, and half sat there waiting to pounce on anything that tried to cause me further harm. I was nervous, rattled and I felt like crap. I fought the urge to throw up more times than I could count. I didn't feel safe turning my back to anything.

When my wife got home, I tried not to tell her what happened because I didn't want to scare her. But when I got out of the shower, she was in the bathroom brushing her teeth, saw my back and gasped.

That's when I told her everything that happened that day. She looked at me wide eyed in disbelief. I couldn't blame her. If it were her telling me, I probably would have thought she was overreacting too.

We laid down to bed and turned the light out. I was still feeling a little green, but not as bad as earlier in the day. I had a puke bucket next to my side of the bed in case I got sick in the middle of the night.

Around midnight my wife and I woke to the bucket spinning in a circle on the hard wood floor. We looked at each other terrified. Oh boy did she believe me then.

That's when the handles on the closet doors also began to rattle. We each grabbed a pillow and high tailed it out of the room. We slept in the living room.

We hadn't been in that house but four months before we listed it. We couldn't live there. The activity was getting worse. Pots and pans moving on the counters, stomping footsteps in the middle of the night, whispers. It was frightening.

I was thirteen when it began. I was elated to attend a sleepover for a friend's birthday. I was fairly new to this school, so it was a big deal that I fit in.

After all the party activities and movies, we were upstairs in my friend Lilianna's room. Some of us were getting sleepy, others were still wide awake and chatty.

Lillianna pulled a Ouija board out from underneath her bed and started giggling. She asked if we wanted to play. Everyone but me immediately agreed.

Most of the girls did not believe in such things but growing up watching ghost movies I was more hesitant.

With all their curious gazes cast my direction awaiting my answer I nodded and agreed. I just didn't want to be teased for being the only one who didn't want to play with it. That was probably my biggest mistake.

The girls sat in a circle and we put the board on the floor in the middle of us. We all leaned over and put a finger on the planchette.

Hailey began by asking the questions. First it was simple things like, "Hello," or "How are you," or "When did you die." None of these brought much of an answer. Everyone but I was beginning to get discouraged. I was elated and ready to stop playing this game.

Sophie asked a question next. "Would you like to hurt one of us?"

We all looked at her in disbelief. Why the heck would you ask a spirit board something so insane. If there was something there it would take that as an invitation!

The planchette finally did move to our horror and spelled out my name. Nichole. I jerked my finger off the planchette as if I had been burned and refused to partake in anything else.

There was the usual arguing of, "You made it move," – "No you did," – "That's not funny."

I sat off in the corner of the room trying to gain my wits while they disagreed between themselves. I was ready for this slumber party to be over at this point. I just wanted to go home.

Mostly I was embarrassed that I let it phase me so much because it probably wasn't real anyways. However, part of me felt uneasy that it had pinpointed me. Maybe it *was* just one of the girls trying to mess with me.

Hailey came over to me and gave me a big sympathetic hug. "I'll put the board away and we can do something else. We can watch another movie and I will let you pick it."

I nodded and watched as she stuffed the board back under her bed. Then I sunk deep in my sleeping bag and tried my best to push the game from my mind so I could sleep.

Around two in the morning I awoke to wetness on my face. It was warm and syrupy. I sat upright in my sleeping bag and wiped at my face. It was blood.

Looking around the room I noticed all of the girls were awake, but Aimee and they were staring at me in panic. Confused, I ran to the bathroom and took care of my bloody nose.

Once I got it under control, I came back in the bedroom to all eyes again on me. "What?!" I demanded.

Hailey gulped, "You were talking in your sleep."

"Like a lot," Sophie chimed in.

"What did I say?" I asked as I situated back into my sleeping bag while holding toilet paper to my nose.

"Couldn't understand most of it honestly," Hailey stated.

"You did say 'Die' before you woke up though," Sophie recalled.

"You guys are nerds. You are freaking yourselves out. Go to sleep." I was trying to keep my cool. Acting tough and unphased by all of it. But to be honest I felt a little uneasy, and not quite myself. Also, I never got nose bleeds. I think I may have had one in my entire life. Weird.

The next morning, I was relieved to finally be home and far away from that board it gave me the creeps.

I took a long shower and laid on my bed reading a book I had started over a week ago. And then there was a loud bang on my bedroom door. Like one loud knock. I went over to the door and opened it. No one was there and nothing was on the carpet.

I shut the door and walked back over to the bed. Before I could lay back down on the bed, I felt it again. Hot, sticky and warm. My nose was bleeding again.

I rushed to the bathroom and took care of it. Why was I having all of these nose bleeds all of the sudden? Stress maybe?

I tried my best to ignore it. I laid back down and held the tissue to my nose with one hand and my book in the other and tried to clear my mind.

I thought that as long as I didn't believe in it, or acknowledge it was weird it couldn't happen. But that's not true now, is it?

The rest of the day was fine and nothing unusual happened. I was beginning to be my bright and cheery self again by bedtime. I was miles from that board, and it couldn't phase me.

At bedtime I turned my tv volume on low as just some slight background noise to keep my mind from wandering to anything negative. I drifted off fairly easily and slept soundly.

At three in the morning I awoke with a startle. I was not in my bed. I squinted my eyes in the darkness and looked around to figure out where I was.

I was in the kitchen, standing in front of the island. I looked down at my hand and I was holding a knife. Immediately I placed it on the counter. That's when I saw the word *die* spelled out in salt on the countertop. What the heck was happening?

I wanted to run upstairs and wake up my parents I was so terrified. But they would think I was making it up or being ridiculous. I swallowed my fear and wiped the salt off into the trash. I would find answers myself.

I ran up the stairs two at a time in fear something was following me. I seriously felt like I was being watched, it was creepy.

In my room I pulled out my laptop and searched multiple articles on Ouija boards. That's when my heart sank. We never said "goodbye" when we were playing with the board. We needed to say goodbye and maybe all of this would stop.

The next morning, I called Hailey and asked if I could come over so that we could say goodbye on the board. She agreed and we did just that.

After we said goodbye, I have not had any more sleepwalking issues or seen the word die written anywhere. I still get chronic nose bleeds however,

and the doctors cannot figure out
why.

FROM THE AUTHOR

At any early age I knew I noticed things that others did not. That I had a sensitivity about me that I could not quite explain.

I loved all horror movies, paranormal movies or shows and grew to love what some others just didn't care to understand.

Through the years I have come to realize that I am what they call "an empath". I feel things that others don't. It could be a place, a thing, a location, or someone talking to me and I just know more is going on then what they claim.

Honestly, I do not do much about this in my life. I've learned to deal with it, and not use it for anything other than knowledge.

I have lived in two haunted houses. This got me interested in the paranormal world and to seeking answers of all shapes and kinds.

I recently started a podcast and we discuss almost everything paranormal, mysterious or unknown. Feel free to take a listen and share your own ghost experiences with us as well!

Forever Haunted Podcast

The Ghosts That Haunt Me with Eve Evans Podcast

A Truly Haunted Podcast

Follow Eve S. Evans on instagram @eves.evansauthor

Made in the USA
Las Vegas, NV
07 May 2022

48570856R00080